# SUE·RYDER FOUNDATION

## A UNIQUE APPROACH TO THE CARE OF THE AGED

# Sue Ryder Foundation

## A Unique Approach to the Care of the Aged

By Martin Beck-Burridge

Foreward by Chev. Charles McDonald & Preface by Andrew Cole

SUE RYDER FOUNDATION: A UNIQUE APPROACH TO THE CARE OF THE AGED

First published in the Republic of Ireland in 2010 by the Sue Ryder Foundation, Ireland

Sue Ryder House, Ballyroan, Co. Laois.

www.sueryderfoundation.ie

ISBN: 978-0-9564633-0-2

Designed by Jessica Tinker

Printed in Italy by Printer Trento

The Garden Furniture
has been presented to
Sue Ryder Centre
by
Portlaoise Lions Club

# CONTENTS

# FOREWARD

**by Chev. Charles McDonald, K.C.S.G., K.M., G.C.H.S.**

The work of the Sue Ryder Foundation in Ireland started in 1978. Our first residence at Ballyroan was officially opened by H.E. Dr. Patrick Hillery, then President of Ireland, in September 1988. However, we had already welcomed our first resident, the late Paddy Boylan, into Ballyroan two years previously in the autumn of 1982.

Since that day in September 1982, so many people have enjoyed peace, security, fellowship and happiness in our residences.

The combined efforts of our voluntary committees in Ballyroan, Owning, Dalkey, Holycross, Portlaoise and Carlow, the Board, shop committees and wonderful volunteers have resulted in the continuous expansion of our work over the years.

Sue Ryder has residences in Laois, Kilkenny, Dublin, Tipperary and Carlow. We also have an ongoing development in Nenagh, Co. Tipperary, which will be ready for occupation in January 2010, as well as several potential projects in Cork, Leitrim, Longford and Kildare.

Our efforts are designed to provide sheltered housing and care for the elderly and for those who cannot cope on their own.

I would like to pay tribute to our founding committee: our Hon. Secretary Mrs Joan Breen and our late colleagues, Paddy Mulhall, Eileen Moran and Bart Horan.

Charles Tweney, present from the beginning, is now our Hon. Secretary and is playing an important role on our present Board under the chairmanship of Andrew Cole. Our auditor Tom Molumby has been a tremendous guiding force down the years and Margaret Dowley has served on the Board since the beginning.

I thank all our volunteers, benefactors and staff for their wonderful support and co-operation which has enabled the Sue Ryder Foundation in Ireland to serve so many people over the years. This generosity has not been limited to our work in Ireland; we have also had many much needed donations for our Sue Ryder

Right: Chev. Charles McDonald.

projects abroad. Money raised in Ireland has been sent out to Albania, Macedonia, Kosovo and Malawi.

We dearly wish that we could do more in the way of fundraising but are so grateful that all our efforts have always been responded to with such generosity.

The Sue Ryder shops serve not only as an excellent way to fundraise, but also as welcome retail outlets for many families on restricted incomes. I am most appreciative for all of the goods and clothes – new, old and used – which have been, and continuously are being, kindly donated by our benefactors. I pray that God may shower His choicest blessings on our friends and repay their unselfish generosity one hundred fold.

We are keenly aware that it is the individual characters who work and live within our residences who make Sue Ryder special. Therefore we have dedicated a section of this book to them and their stories, details of which can be found on the next page; we are just sorry there was not room to include more!

Our challenge is to ensure the enhancement of life for those in our care. Our residences are all not-for-profit and are designed to promote independent living in security, peace and comfort. We aspire to create an atmosphere in which pressures are alleviated and yet where dignity is maintained; we believe this is an environment which enriches lives.

With hope in our hearts we labour to continue the great work and ethos, commenced over fifty years ago by our Founder, Lady Sue Ryder of Warsaw R.I.P., whose inspiration, vision, sacrifice and example I had the opportunity to witness and the privilege to learn from over a twenty year period.

We need your constant support to continue our work providing care that will enhance the lives of our current and future residents.

*Left: Wild Irish flowers.*

*Please join us today in "sharing the care".*

# Residents and carers profiles

ANNE SCULLY

80

BOB & BETTY STANLEY

82

CHRIS WHITE

84

CHARLES TWENEY

86

DEIRDRE KENNEDEY

88

DICKIE CUNNINGHAM

90

GRACE KINAHAN

92

GRAHAM BATEMAN

94

JIM & MARTIN CARROLL

96

JOAN DAVERN

98

JOAN SCHOLFIELD

100

JOHN DWYER

102

JOHN WARD

104

KATHLEEN HALLISSEY

106

KITTY ROGAN

108

LIAM BENNETT

110

MARGRET & VERONA

112

MARTIN BLAKE

114

MARTIN MCLAUGHLIN

116

NED BLENNERHASSETT

118

NIALL CANTWELL

120

RICHARD CONROY

122

TED MURPHY

124

TERESA SHAW

126

TJ & BETTY BYRNE

128

EIMEAR O'HAGAN

132

VIOLET STANLEY

134

# PREFACE

**by Andrew Cole, Chairman of the Board**

I have been a volunteer worker with the Sue Ryder Foundation in Ireland for the last decade. My involvement with the charity all started through a conversation with one of the founder members, Charles McDonald.

Charles shared with me Lady Sue Ryder's vision, which she gained as a result of her experiences tending to the sick and wounded in World War II. This was a prime motivating factor in my decision to join the Irish Foundation. In Europe and Africa Lady Ryder established charities which emphasised setting up palliative care centres. However, the vision for the Irish Foundation was to provide independent residential care for the aged, irrespective of people's means, through donations, income from shops and broader fundraising and this is a vision which I wholeheartedly share.

Lady Ryder and the founding members of the charity envisaged that people's lives could be transformed by establishing community housing complexes which provide residents with a range of services. This has been achieved by developing residences where we can share the care through creating an environment which gives people a high level of emotional and social support.

Our residents come from all walks of life and because of the sense of 'community' within all the residences and continuing their own interests they live lives which are rich and fulfilling. All of our residents live independent lives and many continue their involvement in various forms of charity work in the wider community after joining us.

The Sue Ryder Foundation in Ireland is an independent member of the Sue Ryder International family and the Foundation supports the work of our international sister foundations in Malawi and Albania from our own and Irish Aid sources.

I am confident that our work, in providing and managing cost effective residential units and associated quality care services, will grow in the future. In this way, through

Right: Andrew Cole.

sharing the care in a spirit of best practice, our residences will continue to be available to those who see the services we provide as an opportunity to remove some of the strains of life and to keep themselves young. This can only be done with the continued support of our staff and volunteers, through our relationships with our donors and friends of the Sue Ryder Foundation and through the co-operation of other parties such as the Government.

The development of our Board, through the recruitment of new members with appropriate expertise and experience, is necessary to meet this challenge and I would like to thank the current members of the Board, featured in the picture to the left as well as Margret Dawley, Charles Flanagan, Tom Molumby, Paddy McSwiney and Nicholas McKenna, for all the time they give in helping to ensure that Lady Ryder's vision is kept alive.

Left: Sue Ryder Board Meeting, November 2009. Left to right: Frank Quilter, Charles McDonald, Bob Reid, Pat Breslin, Charles Tweney, Andrew Cole and Martin Beck-Burridge.

# LADY SUE RYDER

## SUE RYDER A WORLDWIDE FOUNDATION

Margaret Sue Ryder was born in Leeds in 1923 to a family of landowners who, from her early childhood, taught her the importance of philanthropy. Her mother, a woman of profound social awareness, would take her and her siblings to the slums where she campaigned for urban renewal and carried out voluntary social work. The 1930s were approaching and with them the Great Depression which would impose economic and social burdens upon populations around the world.

In 1939, aged just sixteen, Sue Ryder joined the First Aid Nursing Yeomanry (FANYs). Later in the Second World War she served in the Polish section of the British Special Operations Executive (SOE), created by Winston Churchill to co-ordinate resistance activities in Nazi-occupied Europe. There she met underground rebels whose courage, determination and sacrifice would have a great impact on her future.

Lady Ryder addressing the Board and others at the official opening of the first Sue Ryder residence in Ballyroan in 1988.

At the end of the War she continued relief work on the continent helping prisoners from German concentration camps and those detained in Allied prisons, bringing aid to those whom the War had left destitute, maimed or ill. She then volunteered for relief work in Poland where she visited concentration camps and met survivors of the atrocities. In her autobiography "Child of My Love" she said of these camps;

*"Each place had its own individuality, atmosphere, tradition – all foul of course."*

She also visited prisons, towns and cities, determined to help wherever and whoever she could, often driving hundreds of miles to see one person who needed her help; the devastation of humanity she witnessed pushed her to do something to alleviate the suffering.

As the Red Cross and other relief agencies were winding down their work in Eastern Europe in the early 1950's, Sue Ryder used a small legacy, credit from her bank and a grant from the German Ministry of Justice to step into the breach. She took on the cause of over a thousand young Poles abandoned in German prisons; a year and eight months later she had organised passes home for all but four of them.

---

Left: Medical care being provided by Dr. Joni Tula, an employee of the Sue Ryder Foundation in Albania, to the late General Kujtim Haliti in his flat in Tirana.

In 1952, with the help of volunteers from more than sixteen countries, she built cottages in Celle, Germany, for men who had been in prison. The project was so successful that Lady Ryder was motivated to build other sanctuaries for the disabled and sick. This commenced with converting her mother's house in rural Suffolk into a place of care for forty disabled or displaced "survivors", or those whom she called "the Allies forgotten friends". Her mother's house became the first Sue Ryder Home and in 1954 the Sue Ryder Foundation was established. She described her new organisation as:

*"an international Foundation that is devoted to the relief of suffering on the widest scale", to promote and provide a multidisciplinary, holistic model of health care based on "the recognition of the unique value of each individual patient, the will to meet the latter's need in seeking fulfilment in all stages of life and the ability to provide health care in a professional and dedicated manner".*

A nurse and doctor conduct a home visit to Isklam Meta, Albania.

Gradually the number of Sue Ryder Homes around the world grew to more than eighty, most of which are in Germany, Poland, Yugoslavia and Greece. They are supported by a network of volunteers and five hundred charity shops. These shops were set up in order to fund her initiatives and are only possible because of Sue Ryder's natural ability to recruit and inspire thousands of volunteers. These volunteers have always been the backbone of the Foundation and Lady Ryder regularly paid tribute to them.

In 1959 Sue Ryder converted to Catholicism and married Sir Leonard Cheshire VC, a Second World War bomber pilot and war hero, who was also the founder and leader of a charity dedicated to the care of people with disabilities. In 1984 they celebrated their silver wedding anniversary in Rome with an audience with Pope John Paul II, bringing with them several hundred of their disabled protégés from different countries. It was their way of celebrating with their "family".

Over the years, the numerous Sue Ryder Foundations around the world have developed and increased the range of care they provide. All of the different foundations are legally independent and most are financially independent, though some, especially the Sue Ryder Foundations in Malawi and Albania, are now desperately in need of financial assistance to continue their work.

Left: Ibrahim, age five, being treated for cerebal palsey by Sue Ryder in Malawi.

In the United Kingdom Sue Ryder Care has grown to become one of the country's leading health care providers, caring for people with disabling neurological conditions or with chronic, life-shortening illness.

On the continent her work extended to establishing homes and services for the elderly as well as for people with disabilities or chronic illness. These services were established mainly in the economically struggling countries of Eastern Europe; Poland, Macedonia, the Czech Republic, the former Yugoslavia and Albania. In Albania Lady Ryder established the only palliative care centre for cancer patients in the country; regrettably the Hospice has since had to close but the domiciliary services are still being provided at the moment.

Sue Ryder also established a domiciliary palliative care service in Italy and in 1990 a Foundation in Malawi was started. Malawi is one of the poorest countries in the world and the people in rural areas have very little

Malawian women, receiving health education.

access to medical care. Sue Ryder is able to provide care for many Malawians who suffer from malaria, epilepsy and asthma.

In the early 1980's Sue Ryder established a foundation in Ireland for the care of the elderly. She wanted to build communities for people to live in which were inclusive to all, no matter what their race, gender or religion. The first residence was officially opened in Ballyroan in 1988 and since this point the Foundation has built other residences in Dalkey, Holycross, Kilminchy and latterly Carlow, with another in Nenagh due to open in 2010. Currently the Foundation has a total of eighty-seven bungalows and one hundred and forty apartments, which will increase to one hundred and ninety-four when Nenagh opens.

Sue Ryder was a petite, frugal woman of astounding vitality, with a tenacious ability to raise funds and who with the help of volunteers formed an international charity that cares for thousands of people across the globe; without her drive, energy and extraordinary humanity the charity would not exist.

Lady Ryder's contribution to the alleviation of suffering was acknowledged when she was granted the title of Doctor Honoris Causa by the Universities of Liverpool, Exeter, Essex, Leeds, Kent, London and Cambridge. She was also decorated with the Order of St. Michael and St. George, the Order of the British Empire, Commander Cross of the

Left: Amadou, age thirteen, who suffers greatly from bone tuberculosis receives care.

Order of Poland's Rebirth, the Order Pro Ecclesia et Pontifice and the Order Ecclesia Populoque Servitium Praestanti.

Sue Ryder was offered a peerage in 1979 and, after thinking about it for some time, she reluctantly accepted the title, most probably because the House of Lords provided her with a campaign platform; she spoke frequently and passionately for human rights and the dignity of the ill and needy.

Sue Ryder is still regarded by the charities she founded and the millions she helped as a shining example of humanity and charity. The foundations she has left will ensure that her caring vision continues to alleviate suffering wherever it is found.

Lady Ryder died on 2nd November 2000 but her legacy lives on in the hearts and dedication of the carers and volunteers, like the ones pictured in this book, who continue day after day to bring hope and relief to thousands of people in her name.

Right: Amadou walks towards the camera.

# THE REPUBLIC OF IRELAND

The "care" that each of the Sue Ryder foundations across the globe provides is directed at different areas of need, depending upon the problems of the country and its population. These areas of need are a function of the different social, cultural and political environments in which the charity operates and aims to understand in order that it might, as we have seen previously, best meet the needs of each specific country.

One of the most influential factors in the development of Ireland as a country has been the changes in its population. Ireland has witnessed an unusual degree of fluctuation in its population over the last two hundred and fifty years. This was caused firstly by widespread crop failures which afflicted the country in the eighteenth century and then later in the nineteenth century because of grossly unjust landowning policies under English rule, when the rural poor rarely had plots which were capable of feeding a family.

Right: The Grand Canal, Dublin.

By the 1841 census, in spite of the awful conditions of the poor, the population of Ireland was estimated to be over eight million. Within ten years the population fell by over one and half million, a terrible effect of the Great Potato Famine of 1845 which saw the massive failure, several years in a row, of the Irish potato crop - the staple food of the poor. This caused a devastating famine and, potentially more destructively, led to huge outbreaks of disease.

During the second half of the century the Irish suffered appalling living conditions, rampant disease, poverty, economic depression and unemployment which, combined with the mass evictions of people from their lands, led to wave after wave of emigration. By 1861 the population had fallen to approximately 4.4 million and by 1961 was down to 2.8 million. The Irish population has yet to regain the heights of 1841. Although the 2006 census revealed that the population had slowly grown to over 4 million, by that year Ireland's society, population, economy and structure had been transformed.

The high rate of emigration during the period of British rule and in the early years after Ireland gained its independence on May 3$^{rd}$ 1921, combined with a low level of Government expenditure over this period, resulted in huge financial solvency problems. Indeed at this point Ireland was one of the poorest countries in Western Europe. The cost to the country was a long period of poor public health and education services and

Left: The General Post Office, Dublin.

limited services for the elderly population, a sector of the population that was increasing proportionally as a result of emigration.

In spite of implementing protectionist policies from this point until the late 1950's with the hope of boosting the country's economic position, the Irish economy remained sluggish until the 1990's. In 1973 Ireland joined the European Economic Union and in 2002 adopted the Euro.

However, it was not until large-scale economic reforms including reduced levels of taxation, incentives for internal investors and reduced economic regulation created a competitive environment, that the Irish economy emerged as an aggressively successful entity which has been named the Celtic Tiger.

During the past two decades the Irish economy has been transformed from a primarily agricultural and rural economy to a modern knowledge based and driven

Left: An Irish Thatcher.

economy. It is dominated by high technology industries in which foreign companies, attracted by generous location incentives, often play a major role; the problem is as costs rise these companies often withdraw. In spite of this the low taxation rates in Ireland make it a favourable location for multinationals and many US corporations claim Ireland is their most profitable location.

Ireland invested very successfully in the development of computer software and is now one of the world's largest exporters of such technology.

Another important new sector for the Irish economy emerged in the light of significant base metal discoveries. The country has three of Europe's most modern and developed mines and Ireland is Europe's largest producer of zinc and the second largest producer of lead.

These improvements in Ireland's economic structure along with investments in infrastructure and education have created an economic power with the sixth highest domestic product per capita in the world, a high level of domestic consumption and a country with the highest

quality of life in the world (according to the EIU's Quality of Life index). This remarkable growth and success was accompanied by a construction and consumer boom, which has given Ireland the reputation of being one of the most expensive countries in Western Europe.

The dramatic transformation of Ireland's economy enabled the transformation of its public services especially education, health, public transport and social welfare, particularly pensions.

Furthermore, Ireland's population structure is not, unlike almost every other developed economy, disadvantaged by an imbalance between the working and retired sectors of the population.

Whilst most mature economies around the world, in Europe, North America and China have falling birth rates and a rising population of retirees, Ireland's birth rate is more than double the death rate. This, plus the arrival of immigrants and the return of Irish people (often with their foreign born children) all attracted by the resurgent economy, has reversed the standard pattern and has resulted in a population growth of 2% per annum, a trend which seems set to continue in the foreseeable future.

Nevertheless, in common with all mature economies, improved health and social care has increased life expectancy and the number of people over sixty-five in Ireland is increasing. The need for services for the elderly has also increased considerably. This was clearly recognised in the 1970's when the Government passed the 1974 Act for the Provision for the Elderly. This Act recognised the plight of many elderly people living alone in rural and urban areas, often isolated, lonely and insecure despite the fact that Ireland's state pension is amongst the top five in Europe.

The situation of the elderly in Ireland was made more difficult during the property boom as the state was unable to cope with the increased demand for 'sheltered' accommodation offering care, community and independent

St. Stephen's Shopping Centre, Dublin.

34

living at a reasonable cost. In response to this, the Sue Ryder Foundation took the initiative and, with the support of the then Minister for Local Government Liam Kavanagh, was involved in the drafting and passing of the Capital Assistance Scheme of 1979/80 which was instrumental in increasing government funding for charitable initiatives wanting to contribute to the provision of accommodation for the elderly in Ireland.

In the last two years the Republic of Ireland has been severely affected by the international climate created by the economic downturn. The country has witnessed a dramatic fall in house prices and a significant construction crash. There is a scarcity of capital as the banks have restricted their borrowing, moreover asset values have fallen and bad debts have risen. The Irish economy contracted by 0.7% in 2008 and worse is set to come as the government forecasts a 9% decline in GNP in 2009. If this is realised it will be one of the largest economic contractions of any western economy since World War II.

The recovery of the Irish economy is likely to be slower than other European economies because of the country's reliance on exports and the massive downturn in domestic consumption. The recession is causing unemployment and income restraints and Ireland now has the second highest level of household debt in the world at 190% of household income. The ESIR predict that recovery will not occur until 2011.

---

Left: The Office of the Taoisech, Dublin.

In spite of the economic gloom, that it is important to point out is not exclusively an Irish problem, the country will benefit from its open economy, an extremely well educated work force and the infrastructure built in the boom years. All these vital assets will be essential to the recovery of the Celtic Tiger.

Perhaps most importantly the Irish people have, in the past two decades, re-created an Ireland of enterprise and creativity that will help to ensure the recovery occurs. In every aspect of human endeavour Ireland's people have made an impressive impact upon the international stage with success in rugby, boxing and many other sports. It is a nation that cares about the arts and culture, so much so that it has created a favourable tax environment for writers, artists and musicians to foster creativity.

The Irish film industry has flourished under the support of the state through Bord Scannán na hÉireann and many Irish actors have had huge success in Hollywood. Ireland has also continued its admirable tradition of free education up to tertiary level for all EU citizens. The country continues to recognise the fact that education is the key to economic growth and a civilised society.

Right: The ruins of the Irish artist Franicis Bacon's grandmother's home in Farnleigh, just outside Abbeyleix. The painter spent some of his early years living here.

Finally, Ireland is a country that continues to provide support for its elderly and retired population. Those who have helped to create the wealth and prosperity so recently enjoyed in Ireland receive a state pension provision that is one of the highest in Europe and is envied by many countries.

Whilst the next few years will almost certainly be exceptionally difficult as government deficits rise and the tax burden increases, it is essential that the government maintains a sense of perspective. Voluntary social and charitable programmes can continue to provide a valuable and essential contribution to the well being of those in need and, if their value to society is recognised, society is the beneficiary.

Whatever its economic state, Ireland remains a green, fertile and beautiful land that is alive with music, culture, architecture and that is home to a gentle, friendly, cultured people. It is a country which is blessed with a landscape that entrances the eye and lifts the soul and which remains one of the most favoured places in the world to live.

Left: Morrisseys, one of the remaining general store public houses; it was previously owned by the late Paddy Mulhall who served on the Sue Ryder Board in Ireland for many years.

# SUE RYDER IN IRELAND

## THE BEGINNINGS

The Sue Ryder Foundation in Ireland was the idea of Lady Ryder herself; she had a vision of a charity that would

*"render a personal service to those in need and give affection to those who are unloved, regardless of age, race or creed, as part of the family of man."*

Lady Ryder joined with an enthusiastic and dedicated group within the Republic to establish a foundation in Ireland. So many people were moved by Lady Ryder's vision that the first committee for Sue Ryder Ireland had sixty members; a group that later had to be reduced to a smaller core team to be more workable! All initiatives of this nature require a few people with drive and determination to carry the project through and this project was no exception and to these founding members the charity owes a great debt.

Although she had never visited Ireland Lady Ryder decided in the 1970s that she would like to extend the work of the Sue Ryder charity into the country. Lady Ryder contacted a friend, a missionary priest Father Kevin Doheny C.C.S.p. from Ballinakill Co. Laois, to discuss this with him. Father Dohery took the idea to Charles and Lily McDonald and the three met early in 1974 to discuss the possibility of creating a charity that would offer a new form of sheltered housing for independent living for the elderly and disabled. The two quickly established a group of people to investigate the possibility of forming a charity to make this idea a reality.

This group included Paddy Mulhall, Joan Breen, Eileen Moran, Anne O'Hanlon, Michael O'Brien, Charles Tweney, Bart Horan, Fran Fogarty, Des Sutton and Robert Johnson who was a solicitor who sat on the Board of the Sue Ryder Foundation in the United Kingdom, all of whom worked together to solidify Lady Ryder's vision and to bring it to life.

The aim of the charity was to help the elderly who remained independent and yet suffered "loneliness, insecurity and inactivity". To help those who live in fear because they resided on their own in areas prone to burglaries and to

Right: An Irish butterfly.

aid those who could not afford to continue living independently because of rising house prices. The aim was also to provide for those who required a degree of assistance for medical or related issues despite being for all intents and purposes independent. It was these people that the Sue Ryder Foundation in Ireland wanted to reach and help.

The plan the charity's early Trustees developed in order to "share the care" with these people was to build residences in which the elderly could live out their lives in their own community with increasing care as required. The residents would pay rent each month which would include the cost of all their overheads: lighting, heating, laundry services, a daily four course lunch, a domiciliary nursing service, a twenty-four hour supervisory service, a community lounge and dining rooms as well as their own fully fitted bungalow or apartment – all of which was to be affordable out of non contributory old age pension.

Left: Building commences at Ballyroan.

These would be residences that people could call 'their home' and which would provide 'care and support' within a community context, friendship as each individual desired, as well as security and independence; the aim being to create a situation where residents could live without pressures but maintaining dignity. These principles remain at the core of the charity's work and the manner in which the residences are administered.

The search for a suitable building to realise these aims began in 1979 in Co. Laois where, other than the excellent hospitals in Abbeyleix and Montmellick, there was no accommodation for the elderly. The founding members were offered an empty three-storey Convent building that was located alongside the Church in Ballyroan, Co. Laois by the nuns of the Brigidine Order who had vacated the building in 1973 to return to the Convent in Abbeyleix. An initial investigation of the building to see if it was suitable to be used as the first Sue Ryder residence in Ireland was carried out by Charles Tweney and several others. The conclusion they reached was that, in view of the poor state of the building's interior and its structural weaknesses, the cost of renovating the building was likely to be more than rebuilding. The Brigidine Order gave the foundation permission to do what they wished with the convent and land, so a completely new design was commissioned to be built on the site.

However, the problem of funding the project remained. The initial efforts for fund raising were very low key and although the charity received a large loan from Sue Ryder UK this was still not enough to begin the building. The turning point for the charity occurred when Senator McDonald retired from his role in the European Economic Community as President of the European Commission for Transport and Regional Development in 1979 and was able to devote a considerable amount of time to the project.

Through his political contacts Charles spoke to the then Minister for Local Government and negotiated the Capital Assistance Scheme of 1979/80 as part of the 1974 Act for the Provision for the Elderly. He wished to pass an Act that would give charities the opportunity to apply for the funding to construct buildings suitable for elderly members of the population who were independent. The Minister entrusted the task to Mr. O'Leary, Assistant Secretary of the Department, who appointed Mr. O'Reilly PO and Mr. Bill Licken HEO to draft the scheme. Charlie McDonald recommended that the scheme take the form of a 'one off' grant or a 'soft loan' equal to the annual cost of

Right: President Dr. Hilliary conducting the opening of Ballyroan in 1988.

a geriatric bed in the District Hospital in Abbeyleix to go towards each unit a charity would build. The original grant scheme provided a non-repayable loan of £16,000 per unit providing the charity complied with the Local Authority's tenancy regulations.

The Sue Ryder Foundation made the first ever application for funding under the 1979/80 Capital Assistance Scheme and was successful in securing funds to redevelop the Convent. This grant scheme remains at the heart of the financial model of the Foundation. By covering these initial costs the government enables the Sue Ryder Foundation to provide accommodation that is affordable for anyone with an Irish non-contributory pension.

The building of the first phase of the development at Ballyroan began in 1980 and ten chalet bungalows, designed by Charles Tweney (a current Director of the Charity), were completed in 1982. Sue Ryder's first Irish residents moved in almost immediately, the first bungalow going to

a local man called Tom Boylan. At the same time Olive Doe S.R.N., a native of Abbeyleix, moved back from Dublin to take up the post of Residence Supervisor.

Up until this point the Trustees had been holding their meetings in the Convent; however, after six years of neglect the building was in a poor state – it had dry rot, no heating and a resident population of mice which would race up and down the corridors! The Foundation's secretary Anne Scully used a room in the old building as an office, accompanied by a very old gas fire for heating, the latter created choking fumes so the cold was often preferable. As soon as the bungalows were finished Anne's office was moved into one of the completed chalets.

The second phase of the project was a two-storey complex with community facilities, offices, a kitchen and dining room and further apartments; this was completed early in 1984. Ballyroan was officially opened by the President of Ireland, Dr. Patrick Hillery, and his wife in 1988, also present for the occasion was Lady Sue Ryder herself.

Through a combination of hard work and the generosity of several Religious Orders the Foundation was soon able to open two further residences at Dalkey and Owning. In addition the Foundation rapidly adopted the Sue Ryder 'model' of developing a group of locally situated charity shops to provide revenue to support the charity. Shortly after the founding of Sue Ryder in Ireland the charity established a number of shops in the country; amongst the first were those in Abbeyleix, Athy, Carlow, Carrick-on-Suir, Kilkeeny, Naas, Newbridge and Portlaoise. After nearly three decades the charity has some nineteen shops that are a major source of income, as against capital grant aid, and an essential part of the charity's economic model.

The shops are run as a separate business and as such they constantly try to improve their market position, turnover and profitability. The shops are a very important source of income for the charity as, although each of our residences are run to be self-sufficient, the income from the shops is the Foundation's main source of additional discretionary income for the improvement of the services we provide. As such the managers and volunteers who work in our shops are an essential part of the 'sharing the care' ethos and we are very grateful for all their hard work.

The Foundation's presence in Dalkey came about because of a direct request to the Foundation from the Department of Local Government for help in providing accommodation

Right: Charles McDonald and Charles Tweney show Lady Ryder around the main house at Dalkey.

for senior citizens in the area who were finding they could no longer afford to rent or purchase homes in such an affluent and popular area. This development, which is in one of the most desirable locations in Ireland, was to prove a massive undertaking for the new Foundation and original estimates were that the building work would cost more than one and a half million pounds sterling. This was the first project ever undertaken by the charity in an urban location and its success was an important milestone for the Foundation.

Our residence in Dalkey is situated in the grounds of the former Loreto Convent which has what a current resident has described as "a superb vista overlooking Dublin Bay". Here the charity built thirty-seven bungalows in the grounds and a further fourteen apartments in the completely renovated and converted main house, which is known as Carrig na Greena House. Dating from the early nineteenth century the house was originally the

home of a well known family of jewellers in Dublin. To this day Dalkey remains a wonderful example of the success the Foundation has had in building an inner community within a residence that is also a part of the wider community of the area.

The next project that the Foundation undertook was a unique adventure that involved the establishment of a semi-independent residence at Owning, in the County of Kilkenny.

As each new Sue Ryder residence was developed a committee specific to that residence was formed to act as a support group. This was the same for Owning, the difference being that unlike the other Sue Ryder residences which are run centrally, the 'local' support group at Owning has independently run the residence since its inception. The following passage is the impressions of one of the early residents at Owning from 1989, describing the set up that Sue Ryder still strives to achieve in each of its residences to this day;

_"The homes are bright and comfortable with large windows_

Left: The Sue Ryder Café in Abbeyleix, 1989.

*that look out onto the lawns and beds in which we have room to grow our own choice of flowers – this is a great facility for those interested in gardening. The homes are all fully furnished and heated. The telephones in each of the chalets are linked to the main house where three caring sisters oversee the smooth running of the house and the chalets. The four course main mid-day meal at the main house is delicious and there is a great emphasis on nutrition. On account of the meals being provided there is very little shopping to be done. They also provide an up to the minute laundry service. The village is nearby, there is a post office where we can collect old age pensions and pay for TV licences without great difficulty. Another popular service is the mobile library that calls to the village every week. The highlight of our privileges is getting Mass every day – there are two churches only a couple of minutes walk from our homes.*

*I would not change a thing here at Owning, it is certainly greater than I would ever have expected."*

Although the committee at Owning will shortly have complete independence, this residence was part of the beginnings of the Sue Ryder Foundation's work in Ireland. From these beginnings the Foundation has grown and developed  and continues to improve and enhance the lives of those who choose to live in 'their own homes' in our residences and under our care.

Inside the Sue Ryder Shop at Abbeyleix, 2009.

In this way we believe we have helped towards finding an answer to the 'problem' of ageing populations. For at Sue Ryder we believe, as AA Gill once wrote, that

*"The old are not the problem – it is the rest of us. We would rather consign the old to a netherworld, a waiting room where they are out of mind and out of sight."*

Rather through helping to build communities, providing independence through care, security and practical support we and our residents not only 'share the care', but create an environment that gives us the benefit of their lives, company and experiences. For it is to these people that we owe a debt, in the words of President Mary McAleese, *"Those who drink from the well should remember who dug it."*

Because one day we will all be old, all facing the inevitability of death. But surely that period of rest, contemplation with and amongst friends and hopefully repose in the love of those whose lives we have helped start, should be;

*"A long moment of success – the pleasure of a race well run, the pride in a family born, nurtured and fledged, a valedictory break on the bench to remember times transcended and misfortunes overcome or stoically subdued"* (AA Gill).

---

Left: The finished bungalows in Dalkey.

AA Gill © The Sunday Times, March 2009/nisyndication.com.

# SUE RYDER IN IRELAND

## THE FOUNDATION TODAY

After three decades of work the Sue Ryder Foundation has grown from its first development in Ballyroan to having a total of six residences in Kilminchy, Dalkey, Holycross, Carlow and, the latest residence in Nenagh, which will open in January 2010.

These residences offer a total of one hundred and forty-four single and two bedroom apartments, which will increase to one hundred and ninety-four once Nenagh is open. The Foundation also has eighty-seven bungalows, each offering self-contained accommodation with bedroom(s), a bathroom, shower, dining room kitchen, and parking spaces. In all our residences we also provide twenty-four hour security, lunch every day of the year, emergency communication systems and care in community.

Although there is a wide diversity of backgrounds, personalities and needs within each of our communities and whilst the residence's physical location influences the shape of our communities there is common thread which is shared by all of our residences. This common thread is not only the care that the staff gives, but also the care that the residents give to one another. Each of our homes offers a unique atmosphere created by our system of care. It is the care that enhances lives, that respects an individual's need for space and privacy but, if wanted or needed, the hand of friendship and concern is always there.

Right: An Irish rose.

# BALLYROAN

Ballyroan was the first of the residences to be built. There are fourteen bungalows in the residence as well as eight self-contained apartments within the main building which also houses several offices, large communal areas, kitchens and a dining room.

The residence is situated in the small village of Ballyroan, next door to the village church which is shown here on the left, on a quiet and peaceful residential road, just a few minutes walk from the village's main street.

The spacious grounds have pleasant grassy areas, there are flowerbeds around all the bungalows and a central green square. There is also a large garden which is surrounded by fields. Each resident can tend the flowerbeds around their home, if they wish to.

All the apartments and bungalows overlook either the central green or the gardens. Privacy is sacrosanct and everyone respects this, but it is not only the staff that residents can turn to if they need support, the residents also look after one another's interests. As in all the residences, there is a very strong sense of community at Ballyroan as one can tell from the animated conversation that takes place around the daily lunch tables!

# DALKEY

Our residence at Dalkey is situated in the former grounds of the Loretto Covent and overlooks the bay on the edge of the old port of Dalkey affording the residents beautiful views across the coast.

The thirty-seven bungalows in the grounds behind the main house are all built around a series of grassy courtyards, bordered with colourful plants and shrubs. The main house, called Carrig na Greena House, has been extensively converted, the original roof replaced and the building has been beautifully restored.

Inside there are a series of thirteen apartments as well as a communal sitting room with sea views and a large dining room. The kitchen and offices are in the central ground floor area, although the latter are being improved and renovated.

The town of Dalkey with its shops, church and excellent pubs is a few minutes walk away. The town has many societies and activities that the residents participate in and enjoy and the residence staff regularly organise opportunities for residents to go on trips to the theatre, to play bridge and to do other activities.

# HOLYCROSS

The residence in the village of Holycross is located by a large green, and is close to the local school. There is a nine hundred year old Abbey just a few minutes walk, along a connected footpath, from the Sue Ryder site.

The grounds are beautifully laid out with trees, lawns and shrubs all around the central single storey complex that contains the office, kitchen, dining room and a large communal sitting room with large windows and views over the gardens.

The small Chapel in the main building is light and airy and has a beautiful stained glass window behind the altar that catches the light.

There are many activities residents can take advantage of in the village and within the residence itself including painting, theatre and social groups.

This residence has an atmosphere of peace and quiet, nestling alongside the Abbey and in idyllic surroundings. It has a vibrant and active community of residents.

# KILMINCHY

Our residence in Kilminchy is situated in the centre of this quiet, small, attractive suburb of Portlaoise. Just opposite the residence is a parade of shops including a pub, restaurants, a chemist and doctors surgery which provide many necessary local services and amenities, augmenting those that can be found in the centre of Portlaoise.

The small chapel in the residence has regular services and there is the main church in Portlaoise which has a large congregation which many of the residents attend.

The residence has a range of apartments which are arranged in three blocks all with three floors served by a lift system. The seventy units include one and two bedroom apartments with generously proportioned sitting and dining rooms as well as a kitchen area which is well fitted with cupboards and appliances.

One of the advantages at Kilminchy is that the residence sets aside several of its apartments for visitors to use when they come to stay, these rooms are enjoyed by many of our residents' guests.

The main central area of the residence has a large, light and airy dining room and a communal sitting area with a large screen television.

Various local activities are linked to the residence and there are many opportunities to travel to the town centre by taxi or minibus.

The residence has a beautiful well-used garden area which brims with flowers as there are many keen gardeners amongst the residents.

# CARLOW

Carlow is the most recent addition to our residences. One of the most important events since the residence's opening was on the 17th November 2009 when we were visited by President Mary McAleese. The photo to the left (supplied by Thomas Sunderland Photography, Carlow) was taken on the day and shows the President with many of our current residents.

The President made a tremendous impression on everyone present, especially the residents and staff who had the opportunity to meet with her. We were impressed by her presence, sincerity and knowledge of the Foundation's works. She is a remarkable lady and we were so pleased that she extolled the work of the charity.

At Carlow we have built two new buildings, both of which are exceptionally well serviced and which provide a total of fifty-three self-contained apartments.

The main building has a spacious community lounge and a large dining room both of which receive a lovely amount of light because of their floor to ceiling windows.

Each building has a roof terrace and the large site boasts several grassed areas, shrubs and flowers providing the residents with a pleasant open space. The site is in a quiet area on the edge of the town and has excellent communication links to its centre. It is on the edge of an extremely attractive residential area and has generous parking space.

The first building opened in January 2009 and already has many residents who have created a vibrant and active community. The second building will be opening in the next few months and will offer the same level of exceptional accommodation, security and privacy coupled with the attention and care of the staff and opportunities for friendship within this growing community.

# PROFILES

## THE RESIDENTS AND THE PEOPLE

## WHO CARE FOR THEM

The people who live in our residences are the sole reason for the charity's existence. It was for them that Lady Ryder and Sir Charles McDonald founded the organisation and as one of the Managers said:

"This is their home, we only work here".

The Sue Ryder Foundation in Ireland has always offered security, independence and care to all who ask for it, regardless of their age, gender, race or religion.

As such, the residents are a diverse and individual group of human beings, but they are all united in their wish to live their lives secure in the knowledge that they are being cared for in a friendly community.

Our core objective as a charity is to continue improving and expanding the shelter we provide.

Right: Residents in the Sue Ryder garden at Kilminchy.

# ANNE SCULLY

Anne was the first employee of the Sue Ryder Foundation in Ireland. Anne grew up in Ballyroan which was where she met Charlie McDonald. When Charlie heard that Lady Ryder "wanted something in Ireland" he agreed to help her start the Foundation and lost little time in employing Anne.

The Foundation's first property was the Convent in Ballyroan. Anne was employed as the administrator for the Foundation and used a room in the old building as her office, despite the fact it was damp and had no heating! As the Foundation grew, Anne managed the central office as well as supervising all the incoming applications for places in the residences which were growing in number. She had very little equipment and no modern facilities, just a single filing cabinet and a typewriter. Despite this Anne managed all the charity's fundraising, including producing posters for every event. On our behalf Anne has orchestrated fashion shows, a golf classic, quizzes and even a singing contest at the Kilishin Hotel!

When Kilminchy opened Anne became its Residence Manager, a position she held until she took early retirement in 2009. Unlike many people who work for an organisation for a long time, Anne always retained a very clear understanding of the ethos of Sue Ryder; "We, the staff," Anne told me, "always have to remember that for us this is only where we work, for the people we care for this is their home."

*"This is an extension of people's lives; it is certainly not an institution or a nursing home. Nobody is treated like an 'elderly person' and no-one is institutionalised"*

# BOB & BETTY STANLEY

Bob and Betty met on Lord Carew's estate where Betty was a dairy and poultry maid and Bob worked on the farm. They fell in love and had a double wedding with Betty's brother in the village of Ballingarry, North Tipperary, in 1954. The couple continued to work on the estate and had a daughter who went to the local school that was at the end of the estate drive.

Shortly after their daughter's sixth birthday Bob and Betty bought a four-acre small-holding and a bungalow. They kept a wide variety of livestock and grew vegetables and plants in two large glasshouses in Wexford. All of their produce was sold to the local community. Bob and Betty supplied fowls, chickens, Jersey cows and turkeys by the hundred to the local market and people. Betty also made cheese for Lord Carew and others. The couple worked industriously until 1996.

In that year they gave the farm to their daughter and came to live in Holycross. Soon after arriving they started working on the land around their bungalow and with the support of the residents they began to make a garden along the boundary stonewall where shrubs and flowers now grow in profusion for all to enjoy. Although Bob is now less able to spend as many hours in the garden as he used to, he is still known as "The Green Fingered Man from Holycross"! Bob and Betty spend their days reading, looking after each other, their gardens and their bungalow.

*"Spending time with and helping just*

*one person is worth it."*

# CHARLES TWENEY

Charles was born in Evesham, Worcestershire, England and studied Civil Engineering at Westminster University. He spent the next decade working with a firm of civil engineering contractors in the UK and the Middle East. Charles then joined Laois County Council and spent six years working in the housing section, which involved in part doing some house designs for the elderly and disabled.

Dr. Bart Horan, a founding member of Sue Ryder Foundation Ireland, sought Charles' assistance in assessing the potential of converting the Convent building at Ballyroan. The building was unsuitable for conversion and so Charles designed and supervised the construction of the first set of bungalows.

A willing group of people from various organisations provided ideas and assistance when designing the scheme at Ballyroan, including the Midland Health Board, Rehab and the Irish Wheelchair Association. The ideas and requirements included raised beds, extended footpaths, small garden plots, electrical sockets at the height of door handles and specific types of switches. The scheme is laid out as a courtyard providing visual contact for the residents to promote an atmosphere of community.

The team that oversaw the design included Anne O'Hanlon (Anne Scully), Des Sutton, Dr. Bart Horan, Joan Breen, Paddy Mulhall, Eileen Moran and Charlie McDonald.

Meetings were held in the convent building and frequently ended when the gas cylinder ran out. On leaving the meeting one had to take care that the door handle didn't fall off and lock everyone in the room!

Charles is now the Chairman of the Development Committee and also Company Secretary. When asked why he remains so involved in the Foundation after twenty-five years, Charles replied that his parents always emphasised that "one should put something back into our community". It is also the quiet satisfaction of not just providing accommodation for the aged, but of giving people "the opportunity to move back into and be part of a community", as he believes that "whatever their station or situation, all people need a community". Seeing the improvement in the quality of life of just one individual, from difficult circumstances, after he or she has made their home with the Foundation, makes it worthwhile.

# CHRIS WHITE

Chris was born in Hackney, East London and went to school at London Fields Comprehensive. After school he studied Classics and History at Surrey University and then went on to complete an MSc in Irish Political Studies at Queen's University in Belfast. Chris then worked for local authorities and voluntary housing associations in London in a variety of roles: housing management, housing development, resident participation as well as policy development.

Chris moved to Ireland in 1999 to work for 'Get Tallaght Working', an employment support organisation focusing on the development of community led enterprises, the most prominent being the Fettercairn Youth Horse Project; this addressed the urban horse issues in Tallaght, Co Dublin.

After a short time he was appointed Head of Development with the National Federation of Irish Housing Associations and worked extensively throughout the country, developing housing projects with both local and national housing groups. He has represented the sector on various national bodies including the Community and Voluntary Pillar of the National Partnership Process, the National Housing Forum and the Deptartment of the Environment Working Group.

Chris was appointed as Chief Executive of the Foundation in November 2006 and having travelled down every road, lane and boreen in Ireland working with parish groups, he told me he feels his experience will enable him to develop the work of the Sue Ryder Foundation, as he will focus his skills and experience on one association, rather than working with four hundred!

Chris has published articles on housing in several journals in Ireland and is a member of the National Federations Development Committee.

Chris is devoted to his young family and spends his rare spare time with his three children.

*"We are a caring charity, we want for*

*all our residents to feel listened to and*

*cared for."*

# DEIRDRE KENNEDY

Deirdre was born in Carlow and has lived in Abbeyleix, Co. Laois, for much of her life. She is married to a farmer and has three children, two sons and a daughter. Deirdre joined Sue Ryder as secretary to the CEO, Charles McDonald, in January 2003. Prior to this Deirdre had worked for nearly thirty years on the family farm and in their butchers. She had also been the secretary for the Heritage Centre in Abbyleix. Deirdre has two sons who live in Dublin and her daughter is a nurse in Portlaoise. Deirdre has now progressed within the Foundation to become the residence manager responsible for our residence in Ballyroan.

When Deirdre first joined the Foundation she told me she immediately realised that Sue Ryder "filled a gap in society for people who want independent living, security, a community and contact with other people. We want the people who live in our residences to have security and a sense of continuity, to know that they are cared for and listened to and above all to feel that this is their home."

On the subject of the impact the current economic situation has had upon Sue Ryder, Deirdre told me she considered "the charity is coping well with the many challenges of the present day economic turmoil that is afflicting our country at present. The important thing is that we have to continue to live up to our ethos and to continue "to share the care".

# DICKIE CUNNINGHAM

Dickie, as she has always been known, was born in Tipperary the only daughter of a family of four children; her mother was a great-granddaughter of the Irish patriot Daniel O'Connell. Her three brothers were disappointed that she was a girl and so they called her Dickie rather than her given name, Ricarda. Two of her brothers were doctors and one an academic historian. Her brother Geoffrey, one of the doctors, lives in his own apartment in the main house at Dalkey.

Dickie is known for her sense of humour, vitality and personality as well as her hospitality. There is a small but prominent notice on her door that reads "Friends welcome anytime, family by appointment"; an accurate indication of her unfailing sense of humour. Dickie is devoted to her family, she has four children, nine grandchildren and two great-grandchildren, all of whom visit regularly. She spent all her married life in Dublin where her husband was a prominent company director of a major pharmaceutical company.

A visit to Dickie's room never fails to lift one's spirits, as she recalls her childhood and memories of a long and full life as well as stories of watching her children's children growing up and taking their place in the world. Thanks to her skill with her 'stable' of four, yes four, electric wheelchairs she visits the town and is often out after lunch seeing friends and shopping, in her words "bad weather is no deterrent!"

# GRACE KINAHAN

*"I believe it is a privilege to live in a*

*Sue Ryder residence"*

Grace's career has taken various paths over the past twenty-five years, from the care of the elderly and terminally ill, to working in the private sector providing treatments and services within the Spa industry. The majority of her working life was spent in the USA where Grace gained valuable experience in both the care and service industries, working for select groups such as the Sports Club LA in the Ritz Carlton Hotel; an exceptional hotel group that has developed great expertise in the area of customer care.

Grace returned to Ireland in 2007 with a desire to work within the public sector again and in October 2008 she was appointed as the founding Residence Manager for our new residence at Carlow in Castle Oaks. The residence was opened under her management in 2009. In many ways, Grace pointed out to me, the Sue Ryder residences are run on the same principles as the Ritz; "you get your food cooked, your laundry done, and so on – you just don't have to pay millions for it!"

When talking to me Grace highlighted that, "a lot of people who live here in Carlow, and probably all the other Sue Ryder Foundation residences, live here because they have suffered hardship at the hands of society or circumstance, and our residences should be a haven for them. One of our most important tasks is to create a community here so that people do feel that this is a place where they not only live but also belong." In many ways, Grace told me, she thinks "it is a privilege to live here."

Grace believes strongly this ethos is very important, because as people get older very often things that have provided belonging in the past, such as being a mother or father, or having a career, are no longer there; children move away from home and start their own families, the time for retirement comes, or your community ceases to exist.

In the face of this it is one of the fundamental objectives of Sue Ryder for our residences to be places where belonging can be re-established, although we also strive to ensure that the human need for private space is respected. Our residence managers such as Grace are fundamental in helping us to create our communities.

# GRAHAM BATEMAN

Graham was born in Cork, his father worked abroad all the time Graham knew him and his mother was a member of the Air Transport Auxiliary during the Second World War. Graham was sent to England at the age of eight as a boarder, firstly to the Horsham School and then to Christ Hospital School. He started learning to fly at the age of sixteen and eventually gained his twin-engine licence.

Graham returned to Ireland to attend Trinity College, Dublin. After university Graham moved into finance and by 1986 he had a successful career on the Royal Dublin Stock Exchange, a considerable fortune, a farm in Meath, and was a member of the Lloyds Insurance syndicate.

Rudyard Kipling extolled those, in his poem IF, who "can meet with Triumph and Disaster, And treat those two imposters just the same". Graham is a singular example of the ability to do this as by 1988 his parents were both dead and by 1990 his fortune, farm and life-style, all earned by hard work and considerable ability were gone and he was declared bankrupt as a result of the Lloyds Insurance crisis.

As this point Graham described to me how, "I had to stay with friends or I was living in bedsits. Eventually, in desperation, I rang my friend Martin Blake who was living nearby and went to stay with him."

Through Martin, Graham was introduced to Charlie McDonald, who very quickly found him a place at our residence in Ballyroan.

Graham has many opinions about the Foundation's activities and viewing them from a business perspective, he does not always agree with them. However, he is absolutely passionate about the care provided by the staff of Ballyroan, the comfort of his apartment and the facilities in the residence, including the lunch! In his words:

*"This place has an inclusive atmosphere and is non-religious, ageist or class conscious; the staff are caring and concerned but do not intrude".*

Graham now lives in Ballyroan on a limited pension. He is always ready to help people and has done so with his friend Martin many times during his time at Ballyroan.

# JIM & MARTIN CARROLL

Jim left the family home in Ireland in the 1960's emigrating to the UK where he found a job working for Dunlop in the huge factory, Fort Dunlop in Liverpool. Jim worked there for more than a decade until the factory closed in the late 1970's. At this point he went into the building industry along with two of his brothers, working all over London for a variety of companies. Eventually he became a 'ganger' and was in charge of a number of men whose role was to lay concrete on large sites as sub-contractors to the Cementation Company.

In the early 1990's Jim, his partner and children returned to Ireland in order to look after one of Jim's uncles who lived in Abbeyleix. His uncle died in 1993 and Jim and his partner separated in the same year. Although this was a difficult period, Jim remains on good terms with his son. He also inherited his uncle's rather isolated bungalow and land near Abbeyleix, a property that had been in his family for more than four hundred years.

Sadly, however, it soon became evident that Jim was unable to live there on his own. Along with many members of his family, Jim suffers from a respiratory disease known as chronic obstructive pulmonary disease (or COPD), that causes a chronic and eventually fatal obstruction of the lungs. Of his seven siblings, five brothers and two sisters, only one sister and two brothers are still alive, all the others having succumbed

to the disease. A young niece used to visit Jim regularly, and she found him collapsed on a number of occasions. In conjunction with his doctors, it was decided that Jim needed to move somewhere that would provide him with a certain level of help and support.

A friend put Jim in touch with Charlie McDonald and Andy Cole and he met with them, visited Kilminchy, and within three months had moved into his apartment. He considers the whole establishment to be extremely supportive; he said he has "peace of mind, security and the benefit of having help very quickly if I need it".

Jim now lives in a two bed apartment with his brother Martin, as he now needs oxygen on a regular basis. The presence of his brother in Kilminchy, makes everything easier for both of them.

# JOAN DAVERN

Joan, originally from Tipperary, is a resident at our residence in Dalkey, and until retiring very recently she was also the residence manager!

Joan very much enjoys living in the Sue Ryder Dalkey residence as it is situated in a very scenic area, on the cliffs overlooking the sea. Dalkey, being a Heritage town, is steeped in history and local folklore and Joan told me that guided walking tours take place every week to different places of interest and that there are also lovely walks to the historic places of Bulloch Harbour and Coliemore.

The residence Joan managed at Dalkey is home to, in Joan's words 'fifty lucky residents'; the residence is situated within walking distance from Dalkey Village and is therefore convenient for the residents to go shopping or to Church services. There are many amenities for the residents to enjoy which are provided by the Active Retirement Association (which has a membership of almost five hundred). Included in these activities are art, aerobics, a book club, bowling, bridge, a garden club, opportunities to learn floral artistry, French and Irish conversation, dancing and to take part in a theatre group. The association also puts on visits to city theatres to see the most recent shows. Joan believes this is a fantastic association to be associated with and told me "many of our residents enjoy these activities, and especially those involved in the painting group who have exhibited, and sold many of their works."

Most importantly for Joan is that Sue Ryder and its ethos fits in so well into the midst of the picturesque town; the Foundation's community is as involved as possible in all local community activities and, now that building work at Dalkey is nearing its completion, Joan said "we envisage even more involvement in the future."

From every point of view Joan is ecstatic about living in such a beautiful, safe, secure and happy environment with wonderful and enlightening companions, as she said;

*"How much better can retirement get than this?"*

*"The most important thing for me is that I have my independence and security. The staff are all helpful, kind and attentive, without being intrusive."*

# JOAN SCHOLFIELD

Born in Dublin, Joan left home at the age of fifteen to join the A.T.S. (the women's army) where she worked on a gun site. After this Joan moved to London but she hated her job there with the BBC so left for Africa in 1967. She lived in Zambia and then Malawi, where she worked for the Attorney General for nearly ten years. Joan also had the opportunity to travel around Africa with her family.

Eventually, she retired to Spain with her second husband before finally returning to Ireland to live in Mullingar. After her husband's death Joan continued live in Ireland but travelled to Europe regularly, often spending time at her daughter's flat in Portugal.

Joan's arrival at Sue Ryder was the result of a chance meeting. "One day", she told me, "I met a friend who lived in Holy Cross and she told me about the Sue Ryder residences, so I went to the Sue Ryder shop in Mullingar and they told me about Kilminchy. I chose Kilminchy because it has guest apartments where friends and relatives can stay", though Joan did tell me she thought the food was better at Holycross!

Joan moved into Kilminchy five years ago. She is interested in current affairs, politics and above all, travelling. This is just as well as Joan's four children are spread across the globe; her son living in Bangkok and her three daughters in New York, London and France. Despite what Joan refers to as "an incident with a taxi", in which she was injured, she is still determined to visit her son in Thailand!

*"I am secure and all the people here are*

*great. A place like this is a Godsend;*

*where would I be without it?"*

# JOHN DWYER

Born in Ireland, John spent his childhood in institutions. The first of these was the St. Michael's Orphanage in Waterford where he lived until he was nine years old. John fondly describes this establishment as "a most beautiful place". He was then moved to another orphanage where he was to spend the next nine years. His experience in this orphanage, which housed approximately six hundred boys, was clearly very unpleasant. John relates that during his time in this institute he spent only five weeks in the classroom, and consequentially was illiterate until he reached his thirties. John was so badly treated that when he was eighteen it was necessary for the Garda to remove him to a local hospital. This period obviously had an immense influence upon John's life, but, a remarkably stoic man, he remains extraordinarily philosophical about his experiences.

John finally "hit the road" in the 1950's and became an itinerant farm labourer. He travelled around Ireland, moving from farm to farm as the work became available. It was on one such farm that John was taught to read by the farmer's children. Work was not always plentiful, however, and John was often forced to sleep rough.

As an adult John was periodically admitted to hospital, including stays in psychiatric wards. Dr Noel Brown, who has since become Minister for Health, spent three years caring for John and helping him in his recovery. Yet, in spite of this catalogue of experiences that would have seriously effected anyone, remarkably John's sense of humour and resilience never seem to have deserted him.

John arrived in Kilminchy six years ago and he has become an important and valued member of the community, spending much of his time tending the flower beds which bring joy to residents and visitors alike.

*"I like to see people relaxed,*

*safe and happy in a comfortable*

*environment."*

# JOHN WARD

John was born in Roscrea, County Tipperary and was educated at the Christian Brothers Secondary School. He joined the An Garda Siochana Garda in 1977 at the age of nineteen. After six months training he was posted to the Cavan/ Fermanagh border at the height of the Troubles in Northern Ireland. In 1982 John transferred to Dublin City and became a detective in the Criminal Investigation Department. He set about his career "with enthusiasm" and was promoted Sergeant in 1993 and Detective Sergeant in 1995.

John met his wife Helen in Dublin and they were married in 1985. After living in the city for seventeen years, the couple decided that their two children would have a better quality of life in rural Ireland and John transferred to the Carlow area. Here he spent the last six years of his time in the force investigating serious crime in the Carlow and West Wicklow area. Whilst this role was a lot less hectic than his previous job in Dublin, John told me the work was just as interesting and fulfilling. John retired from the Garda in August 2008.

In March 2009 John saw the advert for the post of Night Supervisor and Security Adviser at the Sue Ryder residence in Carlow; he applied and was appointed straight away.

When I asked John about his job he told me: "My work in Sue Ryder, Carlow as Night Supervisor and Security Advisor is very rewarding and not as different from Police work as you might think. Taking care of the victims of crime has always been a priority of mine and it is very rewarding to help create an environment where people are relaxed, safe, and happy in comfortable surroundings."

In his spare time John watches and plays sport, especially Rugby and Hurling. He enjoys walking his two dogs in Mount Leinster or on the Barrowtrack and spending time with his family.

# KATHLEEN HALLISSEY

Kathleen was born in Manchester on the 17th June 1929 and lived with her mother, father and sister. At the beginning of the Second World War she became a nursery nurse, looking after the children of the women who were working in the factories. Though hard work, this experience encouraged her to pursue teaching. Kathleen completed her teacher training in 1954 and commenced a long and very happy career as a primary school teacher.

Early in her life Kathleen and her family holidayed in Ireland, and thus began a life-long fascination with the country. School holidays enabled Kathleen to fulfil her desire to travel to Ireland, and for four decades Kathleen and her sister regularly took their holidays in Ireland. In 1976 Kathleen finally moved here and set up in a mobile home in Glasthule. On one of her holidays to Dalkey, Kathleen had come across our residence and after a few years in Ireland she applied for a place there. However, there was no space so Kathleen temporarily moved into our residence at Holycross; when a space finally open up at Dalkey Kathleen said she was actually very happy where she was!

Kathleen has continued travelling and sang with a local choir for many years; she has now turned her attention to painting and attends art classes. Kathleen told me she enjoys the community at Holycross and the privacy of having her own bungalow, she also relishes the many activities that are available to her in the local community.

# KITTY ROGAN

Kitty, as she is known, was born and went to school in Leitrim, in the West of Ireland. Kitty devoted her life to nursing, leaving Ireland in the late 1930's to begin her training in Kingston-on-Thames as a nurse and midwife. In 1943 Kitty joined the Queen Alexandra's Nursing Service and spent the war years nursing in military hospitals in the UK and overseas.

At the end of the war she resumed her career working in hospitals across the south east of England. Kitty had a long, varied and very successful career which she finished as a Matron in the Barnes Hospital in Richmond-Upon-Thames.

On her retirement in the mid- 1970s Kitty returned to Ireland where she lived with her sister, Eileen, until 1999 when they moved into Dalkey. Kitty's connection to the Foundation was her nephew, the late Des Rogan, who was the previous Chairman of the Sue Ryder Foundation in Ireland and whom we all miss.

Kitty is the oldest resident of Dalkey and a very active member of the community. Kitty said that she is extremely happy as she has her independence and can "get out and about much as I like." Everything about Dalkey "is as I wish it to be, it is a lovely place to live, a very lively and enjoyable community, but everyone respects your privacy."

*"All of the staff are wonderful, I cannot*

*say anything bad about any of them or*

*about the facilities."*

# LIAM BENNETT

Liam was born in Portarlington, eleven miles from Portlaoise. As with many Irish families Liam had relatives in the United States; his father was one of eleven boys several of whom had travelled to the USA and stayed. In 1949, having finished school, Liam followed in his uncles' footsteps and left Ireland for New York where, after successfully applying for residence he was immediately drafted into the US Army. He served in Korea during the war, starting in South Korea and going all the way to the 39th Parallel. Liam spent a total of twenty-seven months in Korea, some of which were spent in combat. When speaking of his experiences in Korea, Liam told me, "I was lucky, I got out alive and unscathed."

After his term in Korea Liam went back to the USA and moved to the West Coast to see a cousin who owned a pub in San Francisco. Here he worked in bars and then after seven years decided he wanted to study. He successfully applied for a place at Columbia University to study French, a dream that was enabled by the GI Education Bill. Liam stayed with his uncle during his five years of study and lived off the money he was given under the GI Bill.

Liam had to find work just as the recession was starting, despite this he managed to obtain work on Wall Street in 1957. He survived various layoff periods and worked there for two years but then resigned as he decided he wanted to become his own boss.

Using the opportunity of a GI Loan, Liam purchased a yellow cab at the beginning of the 1960s. He worked as a yellow cab driver for the next forty or so years, building up the business to a total of seven cabs and nineteen drivers. At this point Liam handed the running of the business over to a nephew, though Liam still owns the business and shares in its profits. Once he retired Liam immediately returned to Kilminchy.

Shortly after he returned Liam read Lady Ryder's autobiography and discovered "what a remarkable lady she was: Churchill's favourite spy, she spoke four languages including French, German and Polish and she knew Tito!"

Liam decided he wanted to live in a Sue Ryder residence and applied to move into Kilminchy; he told me he has never regretted the move and loves living here.

# MARGARET & VERONA

Verona Broomfield and Margaret Dowling are two of the Night Supervisors who provide a key part of our care, they are central in providing the security and support that our residents so value. Margaret and Verona have known each other for many years and have worked together in 'care' for a long time both in Kilminchy and before that in another local care home for the elderly. They both work several nights a week and often one day as well.

MARGARET was born in Ballacolla in South Co. Laois and married a local farmer, she and her husband brought up their five children on their dairy farm. After her children had grown up she decided to take up a career in 'care' and started work in a local care home, which is where she met Verona who joined the home shortly after her. Margaret joined Sue Ryder Kilminchy in 2005 as a Night Supervisor and also works days as she likes "to meet the residents" because she told me that at Sue Ryder the residents certainly do "share the care".

VERONA was born in Tipperary and went to school there. After college in Dublin she spent a year with C.I.E. and then upon her marriage moved to County Laois. Verona and her husband brought up their six children on their farm and they now have four grand-children. As soon Kilminchy opened Verona applied to work there and she has done so ever since. Verona shared with me that she loves working in such a friendly atmosphere – "it's like being a mother to a very large family". Verona told me her motto when working at Sue Ryder is "to treat others as you yourself would like to be treated."

*"Although we are both Night*

*Supervisors we enjoy working a day or*

*so in the week so we can spend more*

*time with the residents"*

# MARTIN BLAKE

Martin is a deeply religious man whose experience of life, despite being hard at points, has strengthened his faith. Martin was born into a family that owned both land and horses. His father trained and bred horses on the family's estate and stud farm that was owned by Martin's uncle. The estate was on The Heath, just outside Portlaoise.

Although he was happy when he was living at The Heath Martin recalls how "he was unable to play with the village children". Instead Martin had very strong relationships with many of the family's servants and still recalls their devotion and the care that he received as a young boy during the holidays from the Prep school his family sent him to. One of his fondest memories is "learning his prayers on knee of Chrissie Saunders", a parlourmaid at the time. This belief in prayer is something Martin has retained and the faith he learned from Chrissie has proved to be a strong pillar of his life.

During his time at school the Heath estate was sold and the family moved to Sally Park outside Dublin. Martin studied in Ireland for a year before going to Gilling Castle prep school before going on to Ampleforth. When Martin returned, in his own words, he "took up the life of a gentleman farmer hunting, shooting, fishing, farming and drinking".

A few years later Martin had a breakdown, though he continued farming on his own for a further fifteen years. After this Martin spent the next five years farming with a relative. This, Martin told me, was "a plan that did not work". At this point, after giving a lot of thought to his options and having consulting many advisers, including his doctors, Martin decided to move into one of our chalet apartments at Ballyroan.

Being a thoughtful and contemplative man Martin has a very positive attitude to all of the aspects of his life at Ballyroan. He describes it "a community" and said that he feels "that very strongly, it is 'my' community". The 'community' he describes not only includes the residents but also the staff who, he said, are "our friends as well and are excellent".

He certainly takes a direct interest in all of his fellow residents and is amongst the first to offer help and assistance where needed. Martin is involved in a great deal of charity work and is currently a lay minister.

# MARTIN MCLAUGHLIN

Martin died on the 3rd February 2009, he was a quiet and unassuming gentleman, and he is very much missed by his family and the community of Holycross.

Martin was born in Thurles in 1929 and was brought up by his Aunt and Uncle. In 1942 Martin had a bad accident falling off a bridge and suffered stomach injuries which would cause him difficulties throughout his life. Martin left school at fifteen to work and eventually joined the Electricity Supply Board. He worked on the supply lines, digging holes for the poles and erecting them; he travelled all over Ireland with his job until retiring in the early 1990's.

After his Aunt and Uncle passed away Martin moved in with their daughter, Mrs Joan O'Neill, and stayed in her house for some time. Even after he moved out, Martin remained very close to Joan and her four children Rose, Elizabeth, Joanne and Martin; his sister described him as "a second dad to the children".

Martin came to Holycross in November 1996 after he had undergone several operations. After moving in he had to endure further major surgery and yet remained calm, stoical and cheerful. When I spoke to Martin about Holycross before he passed away he told me "I really enjoy my lunch here", which was fortunate as his stepsister Joan told me: "Martin loved his food but would never cook except for eggs and toast, he wouldn't even buy potatoes!" Martin owned a moped that was his pride and joy; he used it practically every day to go into town and, judging by its appearance, cleaned it as often as he used it.

# NED BLENNERHASSETT

One of three brothers, Ned was born on 30th April 1910, on his parent's farm in Kerry near Tralee in Gortathea. He left school at the age of sixteen to go to Technical School in Tralee for five years. Ned lived at home until he was eighteen and then he moved to Dublin where he joined one of his brother-in-laws in the transport industry. He worked on buses as both a driver and a mechanic for the rest of his working life.

For over twenty years Ned lived with his brother and sister-in-law in Dublin until he eventually bought a house on Villa Park Avenue. Ned met his wife one rainy day when he gave her and her mother a lift in his car to her house number 98 Cabra Road, little knowing this would eventually be his home! They 'courted' for the next two years before starting their married life at 98 Cabra Road where they brought up their family of five children, three daughters and two sons. Ned's family all remain close to him, he has thirteen grandchildren and nine great-grand children!

Ned retired in 1969 and he and his wife sold their house in Dublin and moved to a bungalow in the country, at Ballinlough in County Roscommon, where they stayed until 1990. Their bungalow became an important part of their lives: they renovated the property, restored a large garden, and grew all their own vegetables and herbs. They produced potatoes, cabbages, carrots, cauliflower, lettuce, parsley, thyme, rhubarb, beetroot, peas and black currants some of which they sold; Ned remembered all of this without as much as a pause!

Their feelings of insecurity arose in the late 1980's when there were a few local robberies. However, it was after two sisters living nearby were robbed and one murdered that they decided the lack of security was too great to allow them to stay. After talking to a son-in-law who had seen a photograph of Sue Ryder Ballyroan in a local newspaper, Ned decided to visit and they moved into their apartment in 1990.

Although his wife died in 2000, they never regretted their move. Ned left Ballyroan in 2009 as he had been rather unwell and his daughter Catherine suggested he move in with them when he left hospital. He is now 99 years 8 months old and still extremely bright and cheerful, he told me he was enjoying life and looking forward to making his century.

# NIALL CANTWELL

*"I have no worries; I am well looked*

*after by people who care about me and*

*I have an excellent lunch every day!"*

Niall hails from Dublin and worked in the family electrical business for much of his life but also played the piano seriously from the age of seventeen. Music became perhaps the most important part of Niall's life when he listened to a recording of David Hefcott playing Clair de Lune, a song that inspired him and which he was later to record himself. Although he won several scholarships and was a pupil of both Herbert Friar and Kendall Taylor, Niall admits "the trouble was I started too late".

When his father died in the 1960's Niall and his sister decided to sell the electrical business and retire to Spain together. Here Niall had an apartment overlooking the sea and spent the next twenty-two years playing the piano everywhere he could. In his early years in Spain he performed at Lew Hoad's Tennis Academy and later was asked to play at the Juilliard School in New York.

Speaking to Niall, his passion for music and the arts is very apparent and it is also evident that he misses playing under the Spanish sun. Unfortunately at the turn of the century Niall began to suffer from arthritis in his hands and they gradually became so badly affected that he could no longer play. Although he was granted the Irish State pension, Niall was told he would have to return to Ireland to receive it. Hearing about Kilminchy from a friend, he decided to do so, and moved into his apartment approximately two years ago.

In spite of the dramatic changes in his lifestyle, Niall remains remarkably happy and content. For him, he said, the security, companionship, care and excellent lunches provided at Kilminchy make life so much easier! Niall was also extremely complimentary about the quality of care he receives from the staff whom, he commented, are fantastic at reminding him to take his various medications and at making sure that he attends functions on time!

# RICHARD CONROY

Richard's working life started in the hotel business, he spent seventeen years working in various hotels across Ireland. After this he travelled for four years, working firstly in Prague where he was the Group Operations Manager for a company which ran restaurants and bars and then moving to Shanghai to spend two years opening and running the Dublin Exchange Club. Richard then returned to Dublin to work in security and with the postal service.

Richard joined Sue Ryder on the 1st of December 2003 as the Services Manager at Kilminchy, our largest residence. He worked very closely with Anne Scully, the then Residence Manager, and on her retirement took over responsibility for all our activities in Kilminchy.

Richard is married and he and his wife, Min Yu, live with their son William in Port Laois, near the residence at Kilminchy and the couple are expecting their second child shortly.

Richard's thoughts on his role as residence manager are partly formed by his hotel experience. He told me that working at Kilminchy and "running a hotel is similar; you look after human beings, all of whom are different and all of whose privacy and independence must be respected. In my view the real difference is that we are trying

to build a community and we want to ensure that our residents know that they are only as alone as they want to be – we are here for them all the time and they need to be aware of that, without us being intrusive."

Our resident managers such as Richard, our night supervisors and our other staff are the most vital element of the Sue Ryder Foundation, as they are as the people who give the unique care we aim to provide at Sue Ryder.

*"The Sue Ryder staff aim to facilitate*

*the building of community, but it is the*

*residents themselves who make their*

*community."*

# Ted Murphy

As with a number of our residents Ted spent the majority of his life abroad. He was born in Africa. Though his parents were originally from Liverpool, they had left for a warmer clime. Ted grew up and went to school in Salisbury, Rhodesia. After leaving school at the age of eighteen Ted became the Chief Customs Officer and Ceremonial Head at Port Herald on the River Skiri in Nyasaland. He enjoyed the life and loved the country and told me that he felt "at home there". As a resident of Rhodesia Ted joined the Royal Rhodesian Regiment for his National Service and later, from 1961 until 1980, was a Territorial soldier. In his career Ted also worked as the General Manager of a paper factory owned by the Dickinson & Robinson Group, a British firm specialising in industrial paper bags for transporting tea.

Ted met his wife Nona in 1959 and they were a devoted married couple for forty-five years. In 1995 Ted suffered from a stroke was incapacitated and retired. After nearly ten years of retirement together Nona became ill quite suddenly and she died in Rhodesia at 12.14pm on the 8th of May 2004. Ted told me that it was then that "the light in my street went out".

Ted stayed in Rhodesia until 2007, but the deteriorating political and economic situation forced him to leave Zimbabwe for Ireland. He took the last British Airways flight out of Harare with a single suitcase. Ted then stayed with his brother and sister-in-law who had also been in Zimbabwe, until she suggested that he considered moving to Kilminchy. He made a rapid decision having seen the accommodation and more importantly, having met the people. Ted informed me he could say nothing bad about Kilminchy, as he felt positive about all aspects of the residence. His independence and privacy are vital to him as is the constant support he receives from his fellow residents and from the Sue Ryder staff, all of whom provide him with links to the world.

# TERESA SHAW

Teresa is a native of Thurles in County Tipperary; she was born the youngest of nine children, just four and a half miles from the residence of Holycross. Teresa was educated at the Ursuline Convent in Thurles and spent all of her childhood in the area. Once she finished school, Teresa moved to Dublin where she worked for four years.

After this she moved back to Thurles and worked for Erin Foods until she got married in 1974. Four years later Teresa returned with her family to Holycross, moving into a house that was just half a mile away from the Sue Ryder Residence. Teresa brought up her four children in this home and now has two grandchildren.

While her children were still growing up, Teresa began to work part-time with Sue Ryder and in 1997 she took on a full-time role. In 1998 Teresa became the Residence Manager at Holycross. Teresa's light hand, personality and wonderful smile evidently have a very positive effect on the small community in Holycross. Teresa, along with all of our Residence Managers, is one of the key members of the Sue Ryder family.

Teresa enjoys working at Sue Ryder but in her spare time also takes pleasure in reading and gardening.

*"When we walked into Carlow, we walked into*

*a miracle" - Betty*

# TJ & BETTY BYRNE

TJ was born in Enniscorthy where he lived with his parents until they decided to emigrate to England in 1935. The family moved to a suburb of Birmingham near the Aston Villa football ground. During one of the many bombing raids on Coventry and Birmingham the family house was one of six that took a direct hit; TJ and his family were the only survivors.

The children of the family were evacuated to Ballinabranna, Milford, Co. Carlow to his mother's farm home. Later on TJ, his mother, brother and sisters moved to live with a cousin of their mother's, Peg Foley in the Graiguecullen Bridge area. Peg Foley owned a shop in Carlow which TJ looked after along with her shop assistants. One day, whilst working in the shop, TJ saw Betty out of the window. She was walking her small dog but did not have it on a lead, so TJ tricked it into the shop and when Betty returned looking for her pet he took it to her, pretending he had found it! At this point Betty was thirteen, they were married a few years later - Betty would describe herself as a child bride!

Whist working as a mail order salesman for Cotts of Kilcock in Kildare in the late 1950's, TJ received an inquiry for musical instruments from a group of young men in Waterford. TJ sold the instruments to the boys, then six weeks later he received a letter from one of the boys looking for a guitar. When TJ called in on the young man he was

in rehearsals with the band. TJ was amazed by the "wonderful sound that was coming from this group of very young men." TJ was so impressed he told the boys they should get themselves a manager. The group agreed and asked TJ if he would take up the role! TJ agreed and so the Royal Show Band was born and, in TJ's words, "the Hucklebuck and the rest is now the wonderful history of the Royal Show Band Waterford and TJ Byrne." The Royal Show Band became a phenomenal, practically global, success playing to audiences all over Ireland, England and the United States.

TJ and Betty came to look around our residence at Carlow in 2009 and Betty said to me that she believed they "walked into a miracle". Despite only having lived in the Sue Ryder House Carlow for a few weeks, when I asked why this was, the couple's answers were clear and instant; they talked of security and welcoming residents, as well as friendly and helpful staff. They praised Grace (the residence manager) for her attentiveness, and for giving them "unobtrusive help, time and kindness". When I asked Betty and TJ what they wanted from life now all they both said was "more time". They are a couple who have seen more change in their lives than most and have retained their humour, enthusiasm and positive attitude to life as they enter into its next phase.

132

*"The elderly have made their contribution to our future and now it is time that we made our contribution towards theirs. The Sue Ryder Foundation incorporates everything that retirement living should be about."*

# EIMEAR O'HAGAN

Eimear was born in Newry, County Armagh and is the newest member of the Sue Ryder Foundation. She was appointed in September 2009 as the residence manager in Dalkey, taking over from Joan Davern who has retired.

Prior to joining the Sue Ryder Foundation, Eimear studied Housing Management at the University of Ulster. After this she spent three years with the Cluid Housing Association, managing over two hundred of their units. Whilst this was a demanding role, Eimear found it prevented her from 'working with people individually'. The opportunity to work with a group of people on an inter-personal and regular basis, responding directly to their personal needs, was what attracted her to Sue Ryder.

Eimear has been working in the voluntary and co-operative sector for some time now and has developed a love of working with the elderly. Joining Sue Ryder has been a steep learning curve for Eimear as previously she had mainly worked with general needs housing for families. However, Eimear is very much enjoying the role as she feels it is important work.

Lunch time is Eimear's favourite part of the day as this is when the stories and banter flow; and sometimes even ceili dancing, if you are lucky! Eimear said that she has never received such a warm welcome as that from all the residents and staff at Dalkey.

*"I cannot imagine living anywhere else*

*and I would have to make-up*

*something if I were to complain."*

# VIOLET STANLEY

Violet was born in County Laois, she left school at the age of fifteen to work in a draper's store called Shaws in Mount Mellic; this marked the start of a career which she would follow successfully throughout her working life. Violet moved between various stores in Ireland for the next few years until she decided to follow her two sisters to Gloucester in England. There she obtained a position at the 'Bon Marche' store and was joined by her boyfriend from Dublin shortly after. The two spent six years in Gloucester until they had saved enough to return to Co. Laois and get married. Unfortunately Violet had to leave her job at Bon Marche to get married as the store refused to give her the required holiday to get married. However, when the couple returned to the town after the wedding, Violet reapplied for her job and the store took her back!

In the following few years the Stanleys decided they wanted to return to Ireland to start their own drapery. They searched for a long time for the right business to purchase. Eventually Violet's husband found a potential store in a village near Thurles in County Tipperary. Violet was worried about the investment as the store mainly sold groceries but the couple finally decided to go ahead and in 1961 bought the store which they would run successfully for the next thirty-five years. The couple and their four month old daughter moved into the store in 1963, renaming it 'Stanleys'. Violet moved the store's focus away from groceries and it soon became a renowned drapery. Even after her husband's death Violet continued to run the store for a further nine years. The store's fame spread so widely that an Irish television station made a programme about Stanleys, which was then one of the last stores of its kind in Ireland. Violet still has a copy of it on video!

Violet sold the store in 1966 and moved into Ballyroan a year later. She has settled into her new life well and her daughter visits regularly with her three grandchildren. Violet has become part of the community, enjoying the company of other residents and staff. She also enjoys the gardens and flowers around her apartment as well as the residence's lunches, of which she said "you will get no better in a hotel!" Like so many of the residents Violet cherishes the balance provided by Sue Ryder between privacy and companionship and she still has that encouraging smile that welcomed her customers for many years.

# THE FUTURE

The Sue Ryder Foundation in Ireland was established with the clear objective of providing a unique system of care for those who wish to and are able to live independently but within the context of a caring community. Although our philosophy and ethos has been refined over the years in response to interaction between the staff and residents, its core has remained. At Sue Ryder we do not simply provide accommodation, we provide security, independence and care within a community to all who ask for it regardless of age, gender, race or religion.

We offer support to those who need it whilst also respecting our residents' privacy and independence in a safe and secure environment. This safe environment of a caring community is always a major requirement of those looking to join our residences and it also provides reassurance and peace of mind for the family and friends of those in our care.

Right: Wild Irish butterfly.

During the course of writing this book I have spoken to many residents, their relatives, members of staff and members of the Board and I have been hugely encouraged by what I have heard and seen. I have heard firsthand how residents have "peace of mind" because of the security and care we provide. I have seen their communities in action and have witnessed the sense of belonging and pride that our residents have in their residences; "It is a community here and I feel very strongly that it is 'my' community. The 'community' includes the staff here who are our friends and truly excellent." Walking into one of our residences was described to me by a resident who has recently joined us as "walking into a miracle".

Our aim at Sue Ryder is to continue providing "care that enhances lives" for years to come. However, the economic climate has been transformed in Ireland and the charity sector has been as badly affected as other aspects of society. The economic crisis has meant that the level of Government resources available to charities for new residential developments has been severely curtailed.

These cut backs will not affect the Foundation's current residences, our economic model is established so that all of our residences are self-sufficient. They are also protected by the combination of existing levels of pension, rental and heating support and the income from our shops.

---

Left: The new residence at Nenagh under construction.

This model allows us to guarantee to our residents that their homes will be secure. Providing this security is at the heart of our philosophy.

Nevertheless, cut backs in Government funding will mean a reduction in the Foundation's development programme, but as economic conditions improve we have plans in place to extend our services into new areas where there is a need and where the location is conducive to the level of provision we know that our residents want and deserve. The timing of our new developments will be subject to funding from Government sources and, of course, support from private and institutional benefactors is always crucial for the charity's future.

Our aim for the Foundation is to continue improving the services we offer to those we currently care for. Our residents are united in their wish to live their lives secure in the knowledge that they are cared for in a community but where they can still retain their independence and privacy. We will continue to create environments where our

residents can be in secure in company or in solitude as much as they wish, always knowing there is care at hand for many years to come.

In all of the discussions and conversations I have had with both staff and residents during the process of writing this book, I have learnt that the main difference between the young and the old is the number of birthdays experienced. Our residents have all had unique lives, different experiences and have varied reasons for being with us in their particular residence. They all, the younger and older, of all birthdays and ages, deserve a supportive community, security, safety, privacy and perhaps more than anything, a listening ear and affectionate care.

*It is our responsibility to ensure that that is what they receive from us.*

*All of the time.*

# Would you like to help us share the care?

KATHLEEN HALLISSEY

TED MURPHY

At Sue Ryder we are constantly trying to improve the care we offer our residents and to expand in order that we might extend this care to more of those in need.

If you would like to help us continue to "share the care" you can do so by making a single donation or a longer term commitment.

If you would like to make a single donation please write a cheque made payable to 'Sue Ryder Donations Account' and send it to the address featured on the right hand page.

To set up a standing order to the Foundation please fill out the enclosed standing order form and send it to the same address.

CARLOW, CO. CARLOW

DALKEY, DUN LAOGHAIRE-RATHDOWN

# ARE YOU INTERESTED IN FINDING OUT MORE ABOUT A SUE RYDER RESIDENCE?

NENAGH, CO. TIPPERARY

KILMINCHY, CO. LAOIS

If you are interested in finding out more about any of our residences please either write, call or email us to tell us which of our residences you are interested in and we would love to send you some information.

Address: Sue Ryder Foundation, Sue Ryder House,

Ballyroan, Co. Laois

Telephone: 0035357871071

Email: sueryderfoundation@eircom.net

BALLYROAN, CO. LAOIS

HOLYCROSS, CO. TIPPERARY

# ACKNOWLEDGEMENTS

Jessica and I wish to thank all who contributed, appeared or assisted in the making of this book. Special thanks goes to Charlie McDonald who had the initial idea to produce this work. Also many thanks to all the residents who were kind enough to take the time to tell me about their lives and to be featured in the book; it was a pleasure meeting you all. Finally we would like to thank the Directors of the Foundation for supporting this project. I take full responsibility and apologise for any errors or omissions within this book.

*Martin Beck-Burridge*